You Are Not Your Past

An Inspirational Journey

BY CHARLENE DAVIS, IMH-E®, IFA

DORRANCE PUBLISHING CO
EST. 1920
PITTSBURGH, PENNSYLVANIA 15238

Dorrance Publishing Co
585 Alpha Drive
Suite 103
Pittsburgh, PA 15238
Visit our website at www.dorrancebookstore.com

ISBN: 979-8-89127-832-5
eISBN: 979-8-89127-330-6

You Are Not Your Past

An Inspirational Journey

To Kenneth Robert Davis II

*God has gifted me the experience of his unconditional love
in the physical existence through you.
Thank You.*

PHASE 1

Have you ever heard the phrase "no pain, no gain"? When I used to hear this saying, I would make it synonymous with physical activity such as working out. If your muscles and body ache afterwards, then you are on your way to shaping the muscle mass you desire. It wasn't until recently that I took this perspective and applied it to all aspects of my life.

Growing up, I had a pretty decent childhood. Well, so I thought. As innocent children living in a world full of imagination, we grow with the conditioning as to what the people and immediate world around us starts to form and shape that childlike imagination into a reality that may not coincide with what we thought or have imagined. I grew up in a one parent household, living with my mother and five other siblings. I knew who my father was as he was very active during my childhood up to a certain extent. My father was a contractor that made a decent living and my mother worked full time at a nursing home as a dietary aid. This era was in the early

1990s, so back then those types of careers could earn you a stable way of living. For some reason, that wasn't the case for me. I grew up in poverty. If we did have a place to stay, it would periodically miss an essential resource such as electricity, heat, or hot water. I have distinct memories of staying with close friends, relatives, and even motels as our primary place of residence. This went on throughout my childhood until I graduated from high school. I distinctly remember my mother never wanting anyone to know how bad our situation really was. I commend her for her sense of pride and not wanting to sacrifice her dignity, but that eventually came with a price. How can parents that earn a decent living be so bad when it comes to money and raising their children? It will take years of realization and revelation for this question to be answered.

My parents both grew up in the south of the United States. Both had similar upbringing. My mom's mother passed away when my mother was a child during childbirth and was left with her father who was absent most of the time due to his military status. If my grandfather wasn't out serving our county, he was in a different state raising his other children with his wife. My mom stayed with her aunt and uncle and didn't have much of a childhood. I remember her telling me she loved school so much because it gave her a break from working in the cotton fields. Often, she would have to stay home and miss school to work and help provide for the household. This left her with an eighth-grade education to date. My father grew up on a farm. He lived with his parents as a young boy with many other siblings. His parents decided to migrate up north with his siblings to obtain more opportunity but decided to leave only him in the south with his grandparents. It wouldn't be until years later as a young man that my father would be reunited with his parents and siblings.

My parents met when they were older, after migrating to New Jersey in their twenties, and were married. Not being raised by their biological parents had a great affect on how they parented in the future. My mother had my older sister prior to meeting my father. My older sister's father was a married man. After meeting and dating my father, my mother married him. My parents went on to have four children, my sister and three brothers. A couple of years after, my older brother from both of our parents was born. My father had two sons out of wedlock, then me with my mother, and then another daughter out of wedlock with another woman which made me a big sister on my father's side. These are all of my siblings. Looking back on this, I can conclude that they didn't take matrimony as the sacred oath it is. Needless to say, there were a lot of mouths to feed. Nine to be exact and three households to tend to. There was little to no affection from my parents, and I never heard the words "I love you" leave their mouths until three decades later. I always knew I was loved, but it was never confirmed.

Up until the age of ten, my father was a very active dad. I spent ninety percent of my time with him. I really don't have too many memories of Mom during this time other than seeing her in the evenings when my dad dropped me home from school. He would attend school conferences, talk with my teachers, pick me up from school, and take me with him to his job site. Every time I hear a TLC song, it instantly takes me back to the early 90s and the fresh smell of paint. He was always able to find a carpenter job in the neighborhood.

I was always a great student. So great that most of my primary grades I spent in special gifted and talented classes. The crème of the crème for elementary school. Those days were some of the best days of my life.

One day I eavesdropped on an argument my parents were having. In my lifetime, I didn't have the chance to live with both of them at the same time, but my father was not a stranger to whatever living space we had at the time and definitely the only regular visitor to my mother's bedroom. They were arguing about me. My father was telling my mom that he could no longer take me nor pick me up from school and due to my mother's work schedule, she couldn't either. The school I attended was miles away from our current living space and if the school found out about our address, I wouldn't be able to attend the gifted and talented program. For a while, my mother would drop me off at my uncle's house, which was three blocks from my school. I would have to wake up at 5 AM in the morning because my mother had to be at work at 6 AM. She would take me to the other side of town. I had a key to my uncle's house because he worked night shifts, and I wouldn't disturb his sleep when I came in early morning. I would quietly tiptoe in, fix a bowl of cereal, and watch *Laverne and Shirley* until I dozed off. I then would wake myself up and walk to school. Till this day, I boast about how super intuitive my biological clock was and still is. This went on for a while.

One weekend, my mother and I were driving around on the opposite side of town. All of a sudden, my mother car swerved as if she was a professional driver in the Derby 500. She cut off a car in the middle of the street. The other car had nowhere to go because her car had blocked it off. My mother ran to the passenger side of the car and started beating the passenger that was in the car. A man hopped out of the driver's seat.

"DAD!" I yelled.

Of course, he didn't hear me because I was still in the car and in shock while he was trying to pry my mother's hands off his mistress, who would soon become my little sister's mother.

This is the early 90s so the block boys were hanging out in front of the corner store. A storefront which happened to share the same property as my older sister's dad business who was a barber shop owner. Everyone in the hood respected my older sister's father. He must of gave the block boys the word to break this chaos up because that's exactly what they did.

When I finally saw my other siblings and told them about what just happened, they laughed as if it was nothing. I was so confused. Obviously, they were used to growing up in the disfunction as they got an opportunity to live with both of our parents. As for me, it was not a laughing matter but would soon become the norm.

After this incident, my life changed dramatically. My father stopped coming around altogether. He was absent and I never got to spend time with him anymore. My mom would tell me it was because he has a new family and as a vulnerable child, I believed her. How could he just diss me like this? The next school day, my mother was driving me to school.

I asked her, "Why are you driving me? You're not going to work today?"

She replied, "Yes, I'm going to work after I change your school."

"WHAT?! I have to go to another school? I have to leave all my friends? Why?"

It just didn't make sense. As I aged, the only explanation I give the situation was maybe my mom felt betrayed by my dad's brother for not telling her about the affair. That was the uncle's house I went to every morning and after school.

It was just movie scenes flashing in my mind on that fateful day. A movie that I did not agree to be an actor in. The next scene flashed to me sobbing in my friends' arms as they consoled me while tears left their eyes as well. You would have thought I was moving to a different country the way we felt. Next scene, I'm being introduced as the new kid in the class. Now this school had a gifted and talented program, but because I came late in the year, I had to go into a traditional classroom. Now this school had a reputation for harboring some of the more challenging children from the city. As I was living in this challenging neighborhood, it made sense that my mother had kept me in the other school for so long. Some good, some bad, some in between. I found myself having to switch from a learning, carefree, friendly mode to survival mode quick. I couldn't be my intelligent self. Not in a class with a majority misfits. I had to instantly metamorphize into someone I wasn't but someone who I had to be in order to not get hurt physically. I used to hate going to school and my grades started to reflect it. If I wasn't targeted by the "popular girls" for being the new girl, I was picked on by the same girls for being the new attractive girl that all the boys seemed to be friendly towards. As time went on, I got used to this rugged lifestyle. By the time I was in middle school, I learned to adapt to this new me. I was a product of my environment.

High school was a miserable time. I was the typical cliché cheerleader and that only lasted my freshman and sophomore year because my grades couldn't keep up with my social life and you had to maintain a certain grade point average to participate in sports. So, I clung to my high school sweetheart for the last two years of high school up until my freshman year in college. While all of my friends were getting accepted into universities, the only option I had was to attend the local county college. I figured I would still have the experience of college life that my friends attending universities bragged about. I somehow convinced the academic director of the college to start their first ever cheerleading squad. I made history for this college. I was attending class, going to practices, and cheering for the basketball team. Life was seemly good.

I had my own car that I worked for, worked a part time job, and managed to go classes. I was still living in my city I grew up in and as fate will have it, I couldn't get away from being a product of my environment.

PHASE 2

As usual, my mom worked but didn't have reliable transportation. She had lived paycheck to paycheck for all of my adolescence. Even though my older brother was a known drug dealer that had large quantities of money at the time, his focus was wining and dining the neighborhood doxy instead of helping my mother out. As the oldest brother, I used to expect so much from him. He wanted respect as the man of the house but did not earn it, not from me anyway. I would let my mom drop me off to classes during the day on her days off so she could have a way to handle her to-do list. That didn't last long. I eventually worked and saved up enough money to buy another car and gave her my first car. By this time, I had reached the legal tender age of eighteen and it seemed as if my innocence had left when I entered adulthood. I was so naïve when it came to life. I wasn't prepared at all for what life had in store for me. I started to get involved with and hang around people who encouraged me to indulge in things that I wasn't in my best interest. I started to smoke weed, drink alcohol, date older guys, and slowly but surely, my college career paid the ultimate price for it.

I exchanged my five days a week college career to five nights a week club hopper. I was living the life of a rockstar, except I didn't have the lucrative finances that come with that title. That didn't deter me due to the fact I was young, beautiful, and shaped like a 1960 glass contour Coke bottle. Even though I worked here and there, money was never scarce as men would offer and gift me things and money. Again, oblivious to the fact that they were looking for something in exchange. My physique and passive portrait attracted the good, bad, and the ugly.

I was twenty years old when I met my daughter's father. He was very charming and said all the right things that I needed to hear. I was never told or felt loved growing up so when I heard this in an intimate relationship, I believed it, even if it wasn't the truth. In the beginning of our relationship, I noticed some red flags. My intuition would confirm this to me, but my past experiences made me believe that these red flags were normal. I was used to seeing jealous behavior in male and female relationships throughout the years. I was used to hearing men belittle women and vice versa. I was used to seeing the traditional roles switched and all of that convinced me that it was normal because that's all I had seen growing up. We had good days but the bad outweighed them. The relationship turned tumultuous. He started to become emotionally and psychologically abusive. Knowing his story of how he grew up in the foster care system, I had empathy for him and would reason with self and blame his upbringing on his behavior. Shortly afterwards, my acceptance of this behavior made a clear pathway to physical abuse. I would have black eyes, bruised limbs, and somehow still find myself back with this man. I was afraid of being alone and losing the only person who so called loved me.

When I finally found the strength to say to him that I was ending the relationship, I found out I was pregnant. I had a miscarriage when I was eighteen, so abortion was not an option. He begged me to get rid of the baby and told him I would proceed without him. He eventually came around and accepted the pregnancy, but the abuse didn't stop. It had only gotten worse. Around six months of gestation, we were in a terrible argument. I wanted him to start preparing for something that he was not ready for and was not willing to compromise on. The argument turned physical went he struck me down and kicked me in my stomach. An onlooker called the police, and he was arrested for domestic violence, but it wouldn't be the last time.

During the time he was away, I started to connect with God. I knew him, I worshipped him when I was little, but somehow in this time period, I left him. I knew I needed him and him and only he could help me change my situation.

My daughter was born, and her father came home a month before her birth. I grew up in a single parent household and considering how her father grew up, we decided we would try to make it work for her sake. That was the worst decision I could have made at that time. The abuse became grimmer and now I had to protect myself and my daughter.

After obtaining a restraining order and him violating it a few times, the judge gave him an ultimatum. The next violation of the order would lead him to incarceration. This time he knew it was serious because I was willing to prosecute him which meant he would have a lengthy jail sentence. I was fed up and tired. I wanted to be free from the situation. I had made my mind up that it would be just me and my daughter and I was okay with that. I concluded that raising my daughter in a single parent household will triumph raising her in a two-parent dysfunctional household. Here I was, a single mother on welfare doing the best I could at the time. The domestic violence program that I participated in helped house my daughter and I for eighteen months while I tried to pick up the pieces. The welfare program helped pay for daycare while it was mandatory for me to find a job. Now I had the task of finding a significant job that will hire a college dropout with a few educational credits under my belt.

PHASE 3

I DIDN'T HAVE TRANSPORTATION AT THIS TIME. I WAS RECEIVING three hundred and twenty dollars a month from welfare, half of which went towards my half of the rent subsidy. The food stamps I received only took care of about three weeks' worth of food for the month. My immediate family didn't seem to care about the situation I was in. They kept telling me to leave the relationship I was in and since I didn't, their unwillingness to help was their way of saying, "I told you so."

I was so devastated at what my life had become and again I turned to the only one who I knew who could change my situation. But this time was different. I cried out to God. I was open and sincere with him. I told him I was willing to listen and be obedient. I heard nothing but I felt as if he had said, "okay." I picked myself up from the floor and walked a mile to a local grocery store. I spent the last food stamps that I had on groceries and pushed the groceries home in the shopping cart with my one-year-old daughter happy to ride. It was the most humiliating time of my life, but it humbled me.

The next day, I woke up with an unnatural vibrant energy. I had an agenda to accomplish as many productive things as I could while I had time to myself. My daughter's daycare was within walking distance. I walked to drop her off at school and met the distressed owner of the daycare in the entrance corridor. I could see him scrambling through paperwork as if he was looking for an unobtainable item.

As I signed her in and waved goodbye to her, he asked in a desperate voice, "Do you know someone who is looking for a job?"

I hesitated because he caught me by surprise. He went on to say he was short staffed and needed a teacher's aide. I had worked as a teacher's aide for a short time two years prior and my minor in college was early childhood education. I had studied and earned credits in the field of early childhood education.

After snapping out of what I call a spirit induced interaction, I quickly said, "ME!"

He inquired about my background, and I informed him of the skills and abilities I have to perform the duties for this position. I then walked to the local library, prepared my resume, and came back the same day for an interview. After reviewing my credentials, he offered me a position. After clearing all my background checks, I was hired as a teacher's assistant. I worked at that job for four years. By the time I left, I was the head teacher of my own classroom.

Music had always been my first love. Since I can remember, my dad and mom had me performing and singing in church as early as five years old. My father was in a band and my mother was in a singing group. I grew up in music.

I used music as therapy throughout my life. I would ride a bike across town to record and write music. During this time, I was being managed by a young lady who introduced me to a production company. They were known for their musical talents and had a record deal in the past. I started to record songs at their studio on a consistent basis. I ran across young man there, but a glance was all it was as to I was not interested in any romantic relationships. My manager's house was where I and other music prodigies would meet to produce and write music occasionally. The same young man had appeared as I was entering the residence. He yelled my name, and I did not answer. I thought about the audacity of this stalker! How did he even know my name? My best friend said that she knew of him and was a good guy. I sarcastically replied to her with a nonchalant shoulder shrug. I reluctantly walked towards his truck as he persistently requested my attention.

Before he could speak a word I angrily asked, "How do you know my name?"

Waiting for an extravagant response, I was surprisingly taken back by his next sentence. He said that his cousin, that I had previously recorded a song with, let him hear the record and he was impressed. He followed his statement by inviting me to a studio session with him. I gave him my number and told him I would accompany him to a session under one condition. The condition was that we had other participants with us. It was not unusual for men to lure young women to the studio with a promising music career in exchange for sexual favors and I was not that eager for a music career. He was essentially a stranger that I didn't know, so I wanted to make sure I was safe.

Our first studio session was magical. He allowed me to be the true independent artist that I was. The collaboration was a success not to mention he was a true gentleman. I was impressed. I know, he was a breath of fresh air, but I have come across so many pretenders in my past that I wasn't falling for the first impression. We talked on the phone for long periods of time, days at a time, and occasionally met up for studio sessions. We slowly started to build a trusting friendship. One day while talking on the phone I heard from the spirit. Mid-sentence, this young man's voice faded out and the spirit spoke to me.

I heard telepathically, "You're going to have a son and a daughter with this man."

I continued the conversation. After the call ended, I tried to justify what I heard as a silly thought and immediately suggested to myself that if that was the case, we wouldn't be together. I knew he would be an excellent father because he already was to a brilliant nine-year-old son from a previous relationship he had. I never had a successful relationship with a man, and this would be too good to be true. Somehow I convinced myself I wasn't worthy enough to have loving relationship with a man without it sabotaging it.

As we pursued one another and the relationship grew stronger, I constantly found myself saying or doing things that aligned with my belief of unworthiness. It had been constantly implanted by my mother in my mind that men aren't good, and no man is a faithful man. For a long time, I believed her words. It took forgiveness, trust, and God's intervention to change my way of thinking and for me to know and believe that I am worthy of true love. How did I come to this conclusion? It took time, patience, and faith.

This man had only shown me nothing but respect, love, and kindness throughout our relationship. I started to take off the blinder lens and started to look at life in a whole new perspective. I indulged in my faith. I put God first in all things.

PHASE 4

THE 2008 RECESSION HIT, AND WE WERE IN THE YEAR OF 2009. After moving in together in an apartment in Pennsylvania with the intention to start a new life, we couldn't find work and had depleted all of our savings. My mother asked to rent my apartment in New Jersey. We were able to move back to New Jersey but with limited funds coming in. People did their best to try to emasculate my partner and belittle me. I refused to adopt the mindset that just because we are going through a storm that I needed to let the boat sink. I was determined to patch the hole in the boat and make it to shore. This experience taught me two important things in life. One, you don't give up on yourself when times get rough. You must know you have the power and the ability to create the life you want with intention. Two, some people would love to watch you sink instead of throwing out a life raft to help save you. It's important to know that when this happens, you have to realize that it'll be up to you and only you to save yourself. I thank the Most High God for those hard lessons. I learned how to turn my adversities into opportunities for learning. My partner had a trade background in hazmat and once the market picked back up, he was able to land a career in his trade. The year was 2013 and as spirit once spoke to me, our daughter, and son were here in the physical realm. In 2015, after six years of dating, we tied the knot.

I was a stay-at-home mom. During this time, I was not able to work due to the high cost of childcare and being in a one-income household. I started to participate in organizations and groups that offered free workshops for parents. These workshops provided certificates and CEUs (continuing education credits) that I would be able to add to my resume once I was able to start work again. Once my two young children hit the age when they would qualify for free public preschool, I enrolled them. I was involved in all of the parent engagement opportunities the preschool provided. The particular Head Start my children attended allowed parents to advocate on a council which allowed me to learn so much about advocacy, policy, and procedure within the community. I was so intrigued by how these professional organizations allow parents and families to have a governing voice in their children's education and well-being. They always supported us and treated us with the utmost respect. This ignited something in me. I started to branch out and was getting involved and advocating for other community organizations as well. Me viewing the professionals around me and how it was their career to help empower people inspired me. I thought, wow! I would love to be able to advocate and empower people just like me and the bonus of bringing in income while doing it wasn't such a bad idea as well. Then fear and doubt kicked in. I went back to the mindset of being a college dropout. All of the inspiring professionals around me had degrees and certifications to be able to perform their jobs. The thought of returning to college terrified me. At this point in my life, I'm a wife and mother of three children ages twelve, five, and three. Not to mention I was thirty-three years old. Negative thoughts started to fill my head. I ridiculed myself. The perception of me potentially being the oldest person in the classroom made me feel shameful. The passion I had to achieve this goal of being in the field of advocacy and have a rewarding career overrode all of those thoughts. I just knew that my experiences in life equipped me to be able to help other. I just needed the educational background to do it. I sat my husband down and I talked with him about this passion of mine. I knew that if I decided to enroll in college, it would be a huge commitment and I would not be able to do it without his support. I would never forget the words that he uttered out of his mouth when I finished explaining my plan to him. "Let's do it," he said excitedly. That was all I needed to hear. I decided to enroll back in college at the age of thirty-three. It took me two and half years of attending part time. I scheduled my classes around my children's school schedules, and I was able to find a part time job on campus that I worked in between classes. It was a lot of sacrifice. I learned how to prioritize and enhance my time management skills. I graduated with a degree and was able to start a rewarding career with the nonprofit agency that I volunteered and advocated for mothers and families with similar backgrounds to me. Four years later, I have been promoted at the same agency and now I advocate for domestic violence survivors, the community, and families. I continue to empower women, men, and children to be resilient. I encourage them to know the matter of circumstance right now does not determine their future outcome.

I came from a broken home, living in extreme poverty, to becoming a successful woman who has a positive net worth without any debt. My life changed because I made a commitment to myself. Disciple is the key. I stopped believing in negative thoughts that were embedded in my mind for years and started to nourish my mind with positive input. I read self-help books. I watched a lot of YouTube videos that showed me how to manage time, money, and well-being. Every day I make sure to start my day on a positive note and end on a positive note. Even if I was not able to accomplish what I set out for that day, I give myself praise for doing the best I could have done. Tomorrow is always an opportunity for a fresh start. Sometimes when people hear the word successful, they think of a person having a lot of money, living a lavish lifestyle, or some other important title. Well, my definition of success is setting a goal, preparing to accomplish that goal, and doing your best to achieve that goal. I always tell my teenage daughter who struggles with ADHD and bipolar depression that if her goal was to get out of bed and do something productive for the day, Congratulations! She succeeded. She did the best that she could do for the day and that is something to be proud of. That is an example of how setting mini goals, or any kind of goals, will add value to your ultimate goal.

The message left by Jesus Christ is meant for you, regardless of your religion or whether you consider yourself to be religious. One of many teachings that Jesus taught is that we should exercise careful money management and exercise wisdom prior to making purchases (Ecclesiastes 7:12). To be wealthy is a state of mind, not existence. Meaning, to be rich on the outside, you first need to feel rich on the inside. Take time to really acknowledge this concept. You have to know that the vision and goals you set out for yourself will eventually come forth into existence. Denzel Washington once spoke at a commencement ceremony and he stated, "Dreams without goals are just dreams". Think of the life you want to create for yourself. What does that look like for you? Once you clarify your vision, have faith that it will happen. Faith is often accompanied by belief. Too often we tend to group together the words belief and faith as synonyms. On the contrary, they are quite different. Beliefs can change. Faith involves reliance and trust even in the face of doubt. Have faith in yourself to know that you are a co-creator in this life's experience. Once you inherit this mindset within, it will manifest externally.

We should always be grateful for what we currently have and express that gratitude on a daily basis. Every August, my two daughters get really excited because they know that it's time to go school shopping for September. They also know that in order for my husband and I to provide them with a new wardrobe, they have to clear out their closet with clothing that they cannot fit in anymore. They understand that in order to make room for the new, you have to put away the old. Once the clothes that they have grown out of are donated to a charity or cause, we move forward in welcoming the new. They have been instilled with the gratitude of receiving because they were willing to give. They are reaping what they have sown. The lesson to be leaned here is in order to receive a desired outcome, you have to be willing to give out those feelings of that desire and walk in the desired outcome as if it has already taken place. If you fail to express gratitude, it'll be hard for you to attain more. Gratitude can serve us through the law of attraction. The idea of how like energy can attract like energy simply verifies that as we express the multitude of gratitude, we can surely see the manifestation of more of the same energy coming back to us. As a result, you attract whatever you think and feel.

I could not have accomplished any of my desires without my current beliefs and faith in Jesus Christ. He molded a sexually, physically, emotionally abused girl to a strong, brave courageous woman. He continues to be the head of my life and transforms me into the best person I can be. It is important to tap into your spirituality. Having a connection to a higher intellectual source will benefit you. Why not consult with the being that has every single answer to your book of life? Learning God's word through scripture helps us navigate the world. It opens the door to endless possibilities. Scripture acts as a guide and navigation system to every aspect of our human experience. As I look back over my life and all of the experiences and circumstances I've been through, I wouldn't change not one. I realized that I needed to go through these things to be able to assist others though the same in my future. I am forever grateful for our Father God's mercy and love. He put a calling on my life and that is to serve others. It brings me great joy to help others navigate and assist this experience we call life, and this is just the beginning!

Here are some practical tips to help you on your journey to personal success.

1. Set a Goal – What is it that you want to accomplish? If you need to make a list of mini goals or steps to get to the ultimate goal, GO FOR IT!

2. Repeat Positive Affirmations - Programming your subconscious mind with positivity will create an innate re-

sponse within yourself. Repeating these positive affirmations daily will reprogram your old way of thinking into a new path of possibilities.

3. Believe in Yourself - Don't let people or situations deter you from accomplishing your goal. Failure is inevitable. We will fail at some point in our lives. Use it as a tool for learning and try again. Once you confirm within yourself that you can do anything you think of, the universe will create opportunity and circumstance in your favor.

4. Think Positive Thoughts - The law of attraction states that we get what we attract. Try to always think positive. Positive thinking produces positive results. Negative thinking produces negative results.

5. Surround Yourself with Likeminded People - You need to seek out people who will support your goal in the making. People who have the knowledge or experience that you need can help you navigate and educate you on what is needed in order to accomplish that particular goal.

6. Tuning into Source - It is important to connect with the source that gives us life. This can be different according to each individual. Spirituality involves the recognition of a feeling, sense, or belief that there is something greater than self, something divine beyond human experience. Incorporating a daily practice whether it is prayer, meditation, or spirituality can be very beneficial to one's self-awakening.

7. Mind and Body - There is a direct correlation with how we think and how we feel. Eating a healthy diet can definitely affect the way we feel and the way our body operates. Having a good balance between diet and exercise can produce great positive effects.

Incorporating these practical tips and using them as tools in an everyday practice will propel you into your personal journey to the future. Although what we have experienced during childhood can influence the choices and thought processes made as adults, we have the authority to change the narrative at any point in life we choose. How exciting it is to know and have this understanding! Remember that what we have experienced in our past are lessons that equip us with the knowledge which is needed to better ourselves and help others. Life is not a courtroom, but a classroom. Don't be so hard on yourself and your past choices that have been made. Focus on being the co-creator in your life from the moment you close this book. You are loved, you are strong, and you are here to experience the best of things that this lifetime has to offer. This is your birthright.

www.ingramcontent.com/pod-product-compliance
Lightning Source LLC
Chambersburg PA
CBHW060221170726
48004CB00014B/907